INTERNSHIPS

Tips for Success

Disclaimer / Understand that no internship is alike, and the guidelines for success at each company will deviate substantially. While this guide applies to the majority of internships, there are exceptions, and you should tailor this guide as you see fit to your particular experience. After all, a successful internship is a result of not following a specific set of rules, but being engaged, open-minded, and willing to learn.

Seek your passion

The most clichéd saying to each generation is that you need to find your passion in life, and fuel that passionate energy into a fulfilling career. However, truth be told, this perhaps is one of the most important, if not the most important, piece of wisdom to live by. What you choose to do, the industry you enter, the work you do, will compose one of the largest part of your life, and the satisfaction or dissatisfaction you find from the work you do will affect your physical and mental health.

Take advantage of opportunities to explore.

College, especially during your first two years, is all about exploring your options for those who are less certain on what they want to do, or for those who are already sure of what path they want to take, evolve that interest. Take classes in areas that sound fascinating to you, even if you think it may not be remotely related to your future occupation. Join academic organizations that are unrelated to your major just to see if their subjects may be of interest to you. If anything, at the very minimum, these experiences will certainly broaden your perspective.

If you have a general idea of what you would like to do, deciding on your specialization is the next step. Your major may have different paths for specialization, e.g. business is an extremely broad industry, and finance, marketing, consulting, and entrepreneurship are all various areas for specialization. In other cases, you may be able to better specialize by supplementing a minor, or even in some cases, another major. Talk to your advisor and upperclassmen regarding opportunities for exploring, experiencing, and deciding on specializations.

Ask others regarding their experience, advice, and expertise

Speak with professionals about what they do, and learn the path they took to do the work they are currently doing. If it may be an area you are potentially interested in, ask if you could shadow them for a day. Being exposed to their environment will better allow you to determine if you can picture yourself working the same job one day.

Start interning

Once you identify areas of interest, seek internship opportunities, whether that it be during the summer or part time during your academic year. Internships are ideal for immersing yourself into the industry, provide an impression of your work responsibilities and culture, and serves as excellent experience to speak in regards to at any job interview thereafter.

Purpose

The concept of internships has always been mysterious, confusing, and nerve-wracking. This publication was created for a single purpose: to provide unbiased, honest information when it comes to approaching, exceling, and optimizing your internship.

Unfortunately with the tremendous competition in the job market, (valid) concerns with fulfilling job security have often taken precedence over the true purpose of exposing you with new opportunities and experiences, and as a result, learn more about what you want to do with your career.

It is hoped that with this publication you will be able to approach the logistical components of your internship confidently, so that you are able to focus your energy on indulging in the work, and deciding whether this is where you would like your career to begin.

The Caveat

Internships are wonderful opportunities to gain experience, explore interests, and spike up your resume. However, there are caveats to internships that are important for you to take into account and keep in mind while preparing and interviewing for, as well when engaging in any internship.

Internships typically are a two-way street where while you are experiencing and considering whether this is an occupation you are interested in pursuing in the future, companies are also determining if they deem you a good fit for full time opportunities. As a result, it is natural that a number of companies may try to entice you by providing you with a few perks that full time employees normally would not receive. This may include exclusive intern events, pay bonuses, and even freebies. It is important to keep a straight perspective of what is a typical work experience versus what is simply an intern perk. Intern perks are obviously great, but they certainly should not influence your decision to pursue a certain company or industry.

At the same time, other internship opportunities also risk providing with an invalid outlook onto an industry. The trend of this seems to particularly be the case if you are working an unpaid internship, or if the company is seeking interns for simply errand/paperwork type work. If this happens to you, be careful to neither make assumptions about the industry nor allow it to deter you away from pursuing other opportunities in this area.

Prepare a Resume

Once you know what industry and role you are trying to pursue, the first step to putting yourself out into the intern market is a resume, which essentially summarizes your educational, work, leadership, and organizational experiences, as well as significant honors and awards into one page.

It helps to write down the key points of each significant experience you have had that you feel is relevant to the internship you are applying for. For instance, in product marketing, analytical and communication skills are key to identifying, targeting, and executing promotions to specific markets. A marketing candidate with a leadership position in their university marketing organization may focus on emphasizing how they led a team in executing a community fundraiser, and took steps to ensure that the right people were made aware of the fundraiser. Likewise, in finance, understanding of financial ratios, models, and markets are crucial, and advanced Microsoft Excel skills would certainly be a plus. Thus, an investment banking candidate may mention how they placed first in their undergraduate business program stock portfolio competition.

Use these key points to create resume worthy sentences. This means to be sure to use bullet point phrases, not sentences when describing experiences, and limit your bullet points to three to five. Each bullet point should discuss a different component of your experience, and should begin with an adjective to specify what you contributed. Numbers help to clarify the extent of your impact. Be exact if possible.

For example, if someone was writing about your leadership experiences as Secretary for Alpha Beta Delta for an internship position in public relations, he/she may write the following:

Alpha Beta Delta Fraternity, Sigma Tau Chapter since Fall 2014
Secretary of Executive Board
- Communicated events to over 80 fraternity members via weekly email newsletter.
- Managed social media through Facebook, Twitter, and Instagram in order to publicize philanthropy events to 963 followers.
- Networked with local businesses in order to garner a total of $15,000 in sponsorship.

Communicated, managed, and networked are key adjectives associated to public relations, and help to convey how your experiences and skillset are directly correlated with a public relations career.

Applying for Positions

Once you have a resume ready for submission, begin looking for job postings relevant to your area of interest. Your university career site is typically the best place to start looking – companies with affiliations with your university are far more likely to give your resume submission a chance. Find out when your university career fairs are, and see if companies you are interested in are attending. If they are, be sure to make time in your schedule to attend and speak with recruiters. Making the effort to speak with recruiters will automatically make your name and application more visible in their recruitment process. In addition, a number of companies tend to offer interviews based on the pool of candidates they meet during career fairs.

However, if you notice that the companies affiliated with your university are not ones you are interested in, or do not offer positions related to your interest, be sure to seek other recruitment channels.

Other Career Fairs: If your university is located in a college town, there is a likely chance that nearby universities are hosting their own career fairs. Assuming that your university holds a similar academic standard to your neighboring universities, you may want to consider seeing if you can attend their career fairs as well, which may have companies that may better suit your interests.

Networking Events: Companies often sponsor university networking events to create casual meet and greet opportunities with both recruiters and their full time employees. These events tend to be more casual than generic career fairs, but are just as effective in securing an interview. In addition, meeting with current employees will also give you the added benefit of observing the type of people you may be working with, in addition to learning about the typical workday and responsibilities of a position you may be interested in.

Online Recruitment: Check company sites for open positions, along with other online recruiting sites. However, since online recruiting sites may not give priority review to your resume and cover letter like your university career site would, the chances of your application being chosen for an interview is less likely. As a result, if the company provides you with a recruiter name and contact information, speaking with him/her would certainly put your application at an advantage.

Your resume is the key to getting your foot into the company; however, your resume can only hand you an interview. The ultimate determinate of whether you are fitted for a company is your interview.

To succeed in your interview, it is essential that you devote time towards prep work. This means understanding the interview structure, the type of questions you may be asked, the individuals who may be interviewing you, and the content on your resume. Typically your recruiter will inform you of the interview structure in advance, particularly at least in regards to whether your interview is behavioral and/or analytical.

Behavior interviews: These conversations consist of entirely personal and situational questions. The most common questions pertain to further explaining what you mention in your resume (your education, work experience, leadership experiences, honors), and how you are as an individual, e.g. strengths, weaknesses, situations you were a leader, situations you were a follower, teamwork skills, communication skills.

Case interviews: In these interviews, you are typically given a situation, and asked to verbally analyze and explain your thought process. Your answers in these interviews are generally not as important as the way you communicate your reasoning for your answer. This will allow interviewers to determine the strength of your analytical skills, and deem whether you have the mindset needed for a position. Sample case questions are as follow:

- For a marketing analyst position, you may be asked to provide marketing tactics in order to better promote and increase sales in a local milk brand.
- For a management consulting position, you may be asked to estimate sales based on a new strategy.
- For a financial analyst position, you may be asked to evaluate a stock portfolio, and its trends, and provide conclusions and recommendations.

Technical interviews: Technical interviews are traditionally used to test your knowledge level predominantly for positions that require a specific skillset, whether that be programming in a particular software language, or understanding how to derive and utilize financial ratios. Taking the right classes, and studying for the right subjects can assists with these technical interviews.

Brainteasers: In some cases, brainteasers are also used to test your impromptu analytical skills, thinking process, and reaction to what appears to be arbitrary questions. Examples of such include the following:

- What is your telephone number? Add up all the digits. What does that equal? Now multiple all the digits. What does that equal?
- How many chairs can you fit into the Empire State Building?
- How many chicken wings can you cook in a day with a single pot?

Be sure to also have a basic knowledge of the company before going into your interview. This means understanding the purpose, mission and intentions of the company, along with its company structure, executive board, and financial history. You are expected to have attained a certain degree of understanding of the company when walking into the interview, and some interview questions will directly test how well you have done your research.

To guide you with your research, the following template has been included to ensure that you cover the right topics:

Company Name: _____Abbreviation: _____

Year of Founding: _____Founders: _____

Mission/Purpose: _____

Tagline/Slogan: _____Size: _____

Headquarter Location: _____ Other Locations: _____

CEO/CFO/Board of Directors: _____

Company Structure: _____

Divisions: _____

Company Culture: _____

Earnings Last Fiscal Year: _____

Financial Projections for Coming Year: _____

Headlines in the News: _____

Achievements this Past Year: _____

Outlook for the Coming Year: _____

Interviewing

It is always easy to focus on what a company will be asking you during an interview, particularly since we invest so much time to prepare the best and right answers to questions. As a result, many often forget that interviews are as much the company determining whether you would be a good fit for them as you are figuring out whether the company is right for you.

This brings us to the types of questions you should be asking – there is certainly no definite list, but there are right questions and wrong questions. Let us start by defining what is considered a wrong question.

Wrong questions
- *Avoid basic questions*. Basic questions are questions that you should already have answers to when you were researching the company, e.g. where the company's headquarters are located, the name of the CEO, how large the company is.
- *No negative questions*. While you should be aware of the company's financial health, questions about it, particularly during downturns and recessions should be strayed from.
- *Absolutely no salary demands*. Until you receive an offer from the company, you should not be asking questions about salaries, whether demanding a certain salary, or negotiating what you know to be the average salary offered for the position you are interviewing for.

Right questions
- *Culture*. Questions about company culture are important, particularly given that this is information you can only obtain through talking to current employees or feeling it out yourself while working at the company.

  Sample Questions:
  How would you describe your company culture?
  I have heard that your company culture resolves around a supportive working community. Do you agree with this?

- *Workday*. Questions about a typical workday are acceptable if your interviewer is working in the division or team that you are interviewing for. It will allow you to gauge what your responsibilities may look like if you were to pursue a long-term career at the company. These questions, however, are not recommended if your interviewer works purely in the recruitment or human resource department, as they would likely be unfamiliar with the average workday experience.

How would you describe a typical workday?
What is your typical workday like?
What is your typical day-to-day work experience like?

- *Important qualities*. Asking about the qualities the company values and seeks in interns provides you with some perspective on whether you have the qualifications for the job, as well as the nature of the company. For instance, a company's heavy emphasis on integrity demonstrates that it values an honest, ethical working community.

  Sample Questions:
  What characteristics does your company look for in regards to this particular intern position, and in general?
  What qualities does your company value most in its human assets?

- *Company structure*. Deeper questions regarding company structure are acceptable, and demonstrate that you are seeking to better understand how the company operates.

  Sample Questions:
  Do employees ever move between divisions?
  Do divisions ever collaborate on projects?
  How does the chain of command work? Who would I be reporting to?

- *Mentorship*. Mentorship is one of the most important activities that you will need in your career. Most companies these days have some type of official or unofficial mentorship program, either with networking events, or official mentor assignments. While you may or may not be in a mentorship program as an intern, learning about the company's mentorship program will give you an edge in deciding whether you want to start your career there.

  Sample Questions:
  Does your company have a mentorship program?
  How does your mentorship program work?
  Are there other networking opportunities available?

- *Certifications*. As part of building your career, there will likely be a number of certifications or continuing education requirements that you will need to pursue. Finding out company requirements as an intern not only demonstrates your long-term interest in the company, but your commitment to lifelong learning.

Sample Questions:
Are there any certifications that your company recommends for this type of work?
I am looking to pursue specialized certification upon graduation. Does the company support interest in continuing education?

Thank You Letters

A few decades ago, we would be talking about handwritten, perfect cursive cards stamped and delivered when referring to thank you letters. Thankfully in the twentieth century, we can rely on quick, easy thank you via email.

It is highly recommended that you send a thank you email after your interview. It helps to demonstrate your initiative and interest in the position, and more importantly, allows you to reconnect with your interviewer at the end of the day before next round or final decisions are made.

Note that timing your thank you email is also extremely important. Sending your email too early, particularly if your interview is early in the day, may cause your letter to be overlooked as emails accumulate in the interviewer's inbox throughout the day. At the same time, sending your email too late may limit the effectiveness of following up, as decisions may have already been made by then.

Experience shows that it is most effective to send your thank you email within an hour of the last interview slot. Obviously interview hours may not be easily accessible information – however, here are some assumptions you can typically make depending on the location of your interview. If your interview is at the:

University Career Center – Ask the career center desk how long the company will be present. This will give you a good idea of how long interviews will run for.

Company Office – At a large firm, interviews typically run day long from nine to five. For smaller firms, interviews may also be day long, but can vary given that the candidate size may be smaller.

In your thank you email, it is beneficial to mention significant moments during your interview where you may have especially connected well with your interviewer, as well as points that identified you as a qualified candidate.

For instance, you may want to mention
- Characteristics of yours that translates well for the position
- Experiences that the interviewer shared that was especially impactful and enlightening
- Characteristics of the company that influences your desire to work there

Consider these sample letters when you are writing yours:

Sample #1
Dear Josh,

Thank you for your time today. It was a pleasure meeting with you and learning more about the company.

You mentioned that you were looking for an experienced leader in customer relations. I strongly believe that my background in hospitality, and my past three years of experience in running an event planning business will prove to be an asset to your company as you open your networking event division in the coming months.

I look forward to hearing from you in the coming weeks, and once again, thank you for your consideration.

Best regards,
Jasmine

Sample #2
Dear Josephine,

Thank you for taking the time to interview me today. I had a wonderful time speaking with you, and learning more about the firm – I was certainly impressed that such an abundance of mentorship opportunities were offered to interns.

As mentioned during the interview, I am currently leading and managing my university's student investment portfolio, and I very much look forward to applying my strong communication and analytical skills to your summer analyst position.

Thank you for your consideration, and please let me know if you have any addition questions for me or in regards to my resume at any point. I have enclosed an electronic resume for your reference.

Sincerely,
James

You have interviewed, received offers, and it is now time for you to decide which offer you would like to take. Congratulations! However, before you sign on officially, be sure to ask the right questions and sort through important considerations.

- **What will you be doing, specifically?**
  During the interview stage, you are often given rather broad answers as to what you will be doing. However, when it comes to point when you are deciding whether to sign an internship offer, the company should be able to more or less give you a description regarding the type of work you will be working on.

- **How structured is the internship program?**
  The more structured the program is the better your experience likely will be. A structured program typically offers training, networking events, and mentorship programs outside of the traditional work experience. Unstructured programs, on the other hand, tend to offer less learning opportunities, which results in the intern being used for primarily secretarial work. Learning about the program structure will allow you to identify the level and qualify of work you will be working on.

- **Who will you be working with?**
  How much you learn and your general experience will often depend on the people you work with. If possible, see if you can talk to the manager of the team or department you will be working with. Just from a five to ten minute conversation with them, you will certainly be able to better gauge how your experience will be like.

- **Where will you be working, specifically?**
  Be sure to find out the address of where you will be working specifically. Larger companies, particularly, often have buildings throughout a city, and knowing which building you will be in will allow you to better estimate rent expenses or commute time, and assist with your decision in regards to which offer to take.

- **Is the internship paid or unpaid? If paid, how much?**
  Whether an internship is paid or unpaid may heavily influence whether the internship is feasible and practical for you, particularly if you will be interning in a city too far from your place of home residency for daily commute. If you will be paid, determine if the wage is enough to cover

living expenses in the city you will be in. While internships are fantastic learning experiences, they certainly are not worthwhile to accumulate debt on.

Some universities also provide summer scholarships or grants to cover living expenses for internships. Be sure to check out these opportunities to see if you qualify.

Once you decide on which internship offer to take, promptly notify companies regarding your decision. For the companies where you are declining their offer, simply thank them for the opportunity and your respect for the company. Keep it simple – do your best to keep your relationship with these companies positive. There is always the chance you may end up at the company at some point in your career after all.

Internship Preparation

At this point, you have signed onto your internship – congratulations! After months of resume and interview prepping, you can now redirect you time to learning more about the industry and the company in order to optimize your internship experience.

Obviously, however, what you do to prepare for your specific internship really depends on the type of work you will be doing during the internship. Utilize the connections you made during your recruitment process, as well as any team members that you may have the opportunity to interview with or speak with, prior to signing the internship offer, to find out what you can do to prepare.

Review or learn concepts, and talk to professors who are experts in the field. The best part of being in a university environment is that there are industry experts all around you.

The more prepared and knowledgeable you are about the industry when you walk into your internship, the more quickly you will be able to immerse yourself into the company and your role. In doing so, you will be able to honestly decide for yourself whether this industry is right for you.

First Day of the Internship

Months prior to your start date

Between your sign date and start date, you will likely be receiving some type of communication from the company. For larger firms, there may be background checks, insurance forms (especially if you need drive while on the job), and credit checks (if you will be issued a corporate card). Be prompt in your responses, and keep track of deadlines. Remember that this will be your first impression to the company as an intern.

A week prior to your start date

Your company should have sent you information regarding your reporting location, arrival time, materials you need to bring, and dress code. If you have not received any related information a week prior to your internship start date, be sure to follow up with the company. Typically you will contact the individual or department you submitted your internship contract with.

A few days prior to your start date

Send your manager an email introducing yourself, unless you had already previously contacted or spoken to this individual. In that case, simply follow up with a hello. Also note in your email your start date and ask him/her how you can locate him/her that day.

Consider this sample email, which can be revised to suit different needs:

Dear Mr. Johnson,

Good afternoon. My name is Maria and I will be the intern joining your asset management team next Monday, 6/1. I am thrilled to have this opportunity to work with all of you.

Just to provide you with a little background about myself – I am from New York, but am currently attending University of Abalone in Naples, Florida. I am pursuing a primary major in Finance, and a secondary major in Accounting.

From the information HR provided us, I will be arriving at 8:30am, but will be going through security clearance procedures until 9:30am. What is the best way for me to get into contact with you at 9:30am?
I look forward to meeting you.

Best regards,
Maria Salvadore
(212) 888-9999

The day prior to your start date

Gather identification materials you were asked to bring to work – typically this consists of a driver license, and an additional form of identification, e.g. passport, social security card. It is crucial that you bring the right materials to work, as this will allow you to gain company clearance and badge access.

Review the company dress code, and determine if you have appropriate attire to wear. Otherwise, this would be a good time to invest in work clothes. Spend time to iron out the wrinkles, and to ensure that your outfit appears professional.

Business Professional

For women, this means dark blazer, dress shirt or shell, dress pants/skirts, and dark closed toe heels. For men, this means dark blazer, dress shirt, dress pants, tie (avoid the skinny kind), belt, dark dress socks, and dark polished dress shoes.

Business Casual

Business casual is quite simply a casual take on the business professional dress code. Eliminate the blazer for both women and men, and for men, no tie is required.

Smart Casual

Smart casual can be a bit tricky as there are variances as to the level of smart casual. If you want to play it safe, kick smart casual up a notch, and just dress business casual. It is always better to be overdressed than underdressed. Otherwise, smart casual typically entails looking put together – think preppy, but without the business professional and business casual connotations of dress pants, closed toe shoes for women, and dress shoes for men.

General dress for success tips – as a younger member of the team, you will want to blend in as much as possible in business professional environments. Keep your clothing color subtle and monotone. Black, dark navy, and dark grey are the safest. Avoid bright ties or flash belts.

Your start date, your first work day

The first day is a day of being situated, meeting people, and adjusting to your new environment. Arrive early – punctuality is key and expected. Plan to arrive a half an hour in advance to provide yourself with ample time to handle any unexpected situations.

Keep an open mind, plaster a friendly smile, and don't be afraid to ask questions. You will be working with these individuals for the next couple months, and this is your chance to leave a good first impression. Use lunchtime as a way to connect with new people, whether it is your team, another intern, or a manager you met during recruitment.

If you know that you work a standard eight-hour day (basically if your company does not offer overtime pay to interns), check in with your manager at the end of your eighth hour, and see if there is anything else that you could help out with. Managers are typically very aware of how many hours you will be working as an intern, and will advise you to head on home if you reach the end of your hour limit.

However, if you are interning in a more pressing industry, where your hours do in fact include overtime pay, then the general rule of thumb is that you should leave around the same hour as your manager, unless he/she explicitly recommends that you head out.

Tips for Success

Eat breakfast

Breakfast is definitely the most important meal when you are starting your day at seven or eight in the morning. As tempting as sleeping in for that extra fifteen minutes may sound, you will soon realize how essential a good breakfast is when your stomach starts grumbling at 10am. Make the time to start your day of right.

Demonstrate work initiative

Take initiative and ask for work. If your reporting manager has not assigned you any work for the day, get in touch with him, and offer your help to him. If your reporting manager really does not have any work for you though, ask him if it would be all right for you to offer your assistance to other team members, or other teams on the floor, in the meantime.

Be careful if you end up balancing work from your reporting manager and work from a different person. Realize that your reporting manager's work should always be of first priority.

Ask questions

Do not be afraid to ask questions. Ask tough questions; ask easy questions. As long as the question is appropriate and relevant to the industry and what you are doing and learning, your coworkers will likely welcome your questions.

Interns understandably have little to no work experience in the field. Among even those who have attended the best universities in the nation, much of what interns, aka college students, learn is simply theoretical (textbook) knowledge. Real life situations tend to pan out a little different from what is read in a textbook. As a result, the best and quickest way is to learn from the experienced professional and industry experts that are all around you.

In addition, the operations within every single company vary and contain unique quirks. Part of working at a new company is learning the specific knowledge and skills applicable to that particularly company.

Learn from mistakes

As humans, mistakes are bound to happen. As an intern, essentially a trainee, mistakes are (unfortunately) part of the learning process. When you do make a mistake, however minor or severe, accept responsibility immediately. Do not make excuses, and never blame another person. Taking responsibility at the very least fundamentally demonstrates maturity and integrity.

Apologize for your mistake, and then take personal steps to ensure that you learn from this mistake, and will prevent it from ever occurring again. Take time to understand fully what happened, consult your manager if needed, identify what went wrong, and determine what you will do in the future if you ever were placed in the same situation again.

Gain trust

As interns, trust must be earned. An internship is an eight to ten week interview to determine if you are a qualified enough for the company to trust and invest in you long term. Demonstrate trustworthiness by being grounded in your work, toning down egos, and being genuine as a person. Ask questions when there is uncertainty, and be quick to clear up any misunderstandings.

Maintain confidentiality

Internships makes college students feel all grown up, almost like a real professional, which then also makes college students want to share (and perhaps brag) about the wonderful projects, deals, and/or operations that they are working on. However, these are not qualified excuses when it comes to maintaining confidentiality.

It must be understood that the most valued assets of company, besides its people, is its information, whether it be a client list, client date, or internal company information. How information is used can easily and quickly break or make a company. If valued information was to reach competitors or even the general public, it could be very disastrous to a company's reputation, operation, and profitability. '

Take your promise and contact of non-disclosure seriously. Even as an intern, you will represent the company, and as a company member, it is your responsibility to protect information.

If you are uncertain as to whether the information you are currently handling is considered confidential, assume it is confidential. Certainly it is better to be safe than sorry.

Optimize meals and happy hours

Lunchtime works differently at every company, but if your company is fairly flexible with lunch, be sure to take advantage of the opportunity to use it to network. Eat out with interns or team members, and really use that hour to get to know them. Leave work talk aside, and take time to really hear their story. This will allow you to build a stronger working relationship with them.

The biggest mistake is when interns use lunch breaks to recoup themselves after a long morning of work, meetings, and discussions. With the limited time you have within an internship to get to know the company and its people, it is crucial that you spend every minute, and every opportunity, to network.

If you are of age, attend company happy hours, which offer a casual, low-stress environment to hang out with coworkers. Word of caution, however, know your tolerance, and limit your intake. Getting drunk, throwing up, or saying things that you will easily regret are not impressions you want to ever make among colleagues.

Always be positive

The chances of encountering mundane and tedious work at any job are pretty much guaranteed. As an intern, and even a first or second year, a large portion of what you do will probably be mundane – after all, you are the lowest on the ladder, and you need to learn to handle it.

The best way to be positive in these situations is to focus on how your work contributes to the overall functions of the company, no matter how menial. Every task, regardless of how simple it is, is significant to the company in some way. Otherwise, you certainly would not be asked to perform it.

Remind yourself as an intern that your internship is more than what you are currently doing with your specific role. It is about observing the industry, and finding out whether this is the direction you want to take your career, or elsewhere. Spend time gathering insight, and you will see the value in what you are doing.

Expect evaluations

You will probably be given at least one performance evaluation, if not two. Companies provide an outline of what you will be evaluated on, and you can use this outline as a guideline for expectations.

To avoid any evaluation surprises, and to also ensure high performance standards, it may be helpful for you to review your performance with your manager every couple of weeks. Asking for feedback again allows you to demonstrate self-initiative, and will also allow you consistently reevaluate your work approach and adjust your performance accordingly.

As for evaluations themselves, you may or may not receive your scores. If you do not receive your scores automatically, ask your manager if it would be possible for you to sit down with him/her to review them.

Realize that evaluations are always subjective, and what is written on there might not necessarily be what you want to hear. Do keep an open mind, and if needed, ask for more specific examples and recommended steps to further develop yourself. No one is perfect, and constructive feedback in truth demonstrates that your evaluator is interested in seeing you grow more than anything.

If you feel that your evaluation was unfairly scored, avoid getting defensive. Instead, try to reflect and understand why you may have been given these scores. Discuss with your evaluator, and explain why your scores surprised you.

Stay healthy
In order to succeed in what you do, you need to stay healthy. As devoted you are to your internship, you need to be scheduling enough time for sleep, exercise, and eating well. If you are engaged in a demanding internship, this will be particularly difficult since approximately 90% of your time will be spent at the office, and any meals will likely come from a delivery menu.

At the very least, choose as nutritious of a meal as possible. Stick to brain food, high in nutrients, and low in fat and sodium.

No vacation days
You must be committed to the length of your internship to its entirety. There are no vacation days. Given how little an internship term is, it is important to embrace and maximize every minute of it. However, if you do have a pre-committed significant event, e.g. family wedding, or an emergency situation you must address, be sure to inform your manager immediately.

Limit social media

While you are at work, limit your social media intake. Believe it or not, a number of companies actually run trackers on their network and computers, which monitors the sites a person visits. Although this information is not extensively looked at, it is information that is readily out there and available. Furthermore, if your manager or coworker catches you on social media, that may add a negative impression.

If you need a break from your word document or excel page, limit yourself to professional/industry-related sites instead. At the very least, this would look far more professional.

Avoid dating coworkers

At some point, you may be faced with the decision of whether to get involved with a coworker. General rule of thumb to play safe – avoid it altogether. Politely decline, and make it clear that you do not date coworkers. Emphasize that your career is of priority to you.

If you do get involved with anyone, be prepared for office gossip and potentially some office drama to precipitate. Remember that you are an intern at this time, and your internship serves as a summer-long interview. You certainly do not want your performance review to entice any non-professional comments.

Create a Network Directory

Over the course of your undergraduate career, you will be meeting a number of professionals from a wide variety of industries, and it is to your advantage to begin using these opportunities to begin building your professional network as soon as possible. However, as you meet more and more professionals, it will become increasingly difficult to recall names, and certainly there is nothing more embarrassing than to have forgotten one's name, particularly if they remember yours.

Begin by keeping a log, and writing down names to track the individuals you meet.

Key information to write down:

- First, Last Name
- Date of Encounter
- Industry
- Company/Position
- Your impression of him/her
- Facts you learned about them
- Picture (if feasible, otherwise note significant facial characteristics that will allow you to better recognize them)

This directory can then be used to reach out to industry individuals whenever you have a career question or need, as well as when you head into networking events with these same individuals. Your ability to recognize, address individuals, and recall facts will cause everyone to naturally assume that you have a photographic memory.

Admittedly this technique may sound a bit overboard at first, but in truth, this is the secret to transforming your professional network, and developing you into an impressive networker.

How to Network Well

Be a professional. Be put together, and always be the best version of you. Being positive, confident, friendly, and mature will go a long way.

Open body language is key when you are meeting new people.

- **Smile** – smiling is a friendly gesture, and shows that you are attuned to your surrounding.
- **Open arms** – avoid crossing your arms, which often makes you appear cold and closed for conversations. Having your arms in front of your body, in a way, creates a barrier between you and others.
- **Straight legs** – similar to crossed arms, crossed legs also create an unnecessary barrier between you and the other person.
- **Lean forward** – particularly if you are sitting down in chairs, leaning slight forward in the direction towards the person who is speaking will suggest genuine interest in the conversation.
- **Nod**– nodding during conversations signal that you are engaged with the other person and what they are saying.
- **Eye contact** – look at the other person in the eye when you are talking to them. This helps in making you seem more confident and keeps the other person engaged to what you are saying as well.

In addition, it is important that you pick the right opportunities to network:

- **Utilize your alumni network**.
  Your university alumni network is the best place to start building a network, and to bridge you with other individuals in the industry. Utilize your university's alumni directory, and be aware of upcoming alumni events.

- **Attend networking events**.
  Find out more information from your university regarding networking events held by companies on your campus – there will likely be wide variety of events particularly during recruitment seasons in early Fall and early Spring, ranging from career fairs, informational sessions, hackathons, mocktail sessions, to dinners.

  Look up other networking events in the area. Nearby universities may provide you with additional opportunities, assuming that they do not close their sessions to only their university students. If you are living in a larger metropolitan area, occasionally the government may sponsor career fairs and other general networking opportunities.

Maintaining Your Network

Networking is not about meeting the rich and famous. Networking is not about collecting business cards. Networking, even at its core, is not just about meeting people. So what is networking?

Networking is about meeting people, getting to know them, and building long-term relationships. Relationships are established through good conversations and investing time. These relationships will in turn allow you to establish a viable and valuable network as you build your career.

Work is required on your part to build a strong and sustainable professional network. Meeting the person and initial introductions are easy, but getting to know the person and seriously keeping in touch is far more difficult. With school, work, extracurricular activities, and maintaining a social life, there always seems to be so little time for networking.

Here are our recommendations:

- **Keep it casual, and schedule for coffee.** Dinners always seem to take too much time, and are often too formal especially if you do not know the person that well. Lunches, even quick ones, require at least one precious hour to be sacrificed. Coffee keeps everything casual with little time commitment. Everyone is busy, but no one is ever too busy for a quick cup of joe.

- **Send holiday greetings.** Holidays are an excellent time to send a little note to your network, whether it is via email or a snail mail note. Either way it allows you to casually reach out to others and keep yourself memorable. Plus everyone loves a good, sincere holiday greeting.

- **Send articles that may be of interest to individuals within your network.** Doing this shows that you remember these individuals, and perhaps recall specific facts from conversations you had with them. In addition, this once again heads to keep you memorable.

General benefits of having a strong professional network:

- You are able to seek unique industry information that extends beyond your expertise or knowledge. This is helpful both when you are studying in school, as well as once you graduate and specialize in a field.
- You are able to gain career insight among a vast amount of industries. As you explore industries to find the area you want to start your career in,

working professionals are the ones who can best provide you with an accurate picture of what working in certain industries look like.

- You can gain an advantage in the application process for internships and full time jobs if an individual within your network and working at that company is willing to vouch for you.
- You will find lifelong mentors within your network that will be able to advise you as you move up in your career.

Do understand, however, that your professional network is a give and take relationship, whether you are younger or older, the mentee or mentor, the inexperience or experienced. This is especially true once you graduate, begin working full time, and specialize in industry knowledge.

Wrapping Up Your Internship

You are approaching the end of your internship at this point – hopefully it has been an experience of a lifetime that has given you some insight on the direction you want to take your career.

At this time, it is important that you take steps to end your internship on a strong note, with a larger professional network, greater experience, and lifelong mentors.

Write thank you letters
Handwrite thank you letters to thank every person that has impacted your internship experience. It helps to be specific in what you are thanking him/her for, whether it be for teaching you the ropes the first day, mentoring you on where to take your career next, or the industry knowledge he/she shared with you.

The formality of these messages depends on your relationship with the person and the company culture. Lean on the professional side if there is any uncertainty.

Gift or no gift
A personal letter always says more than a gift – however, if your company does allow gifting, it is an option. Do look into your company policies to ensure that you are following protocol. Most have a limit as to the amount gifts may cost. If you are looking to keep it simple, include a chocolate bar in each of your card, or bring in a box of cookies or donuts for your team to share.

Keep in touch with coworkers
Now that your internship is wrapping up, you will soon need to make special effort to stay connected with your colleagues. Gather their email addresses and use professional networks like LinkedIn to keep in touch. Stray away from Facebook as a professional networking tool unless you are certain that he/she is fine with such an informal, casual form of networking.

It also helps to identify and confirm with specific individuals in regards to letters of recommendations in the future. Regardless of whether you will be continuing to pursue this industry, letters of recommendations from any employers helps to validate your abilities and level of performance.

In the exit process of your internship, be sure to be thorough. Your desk should be left exactly the same way you found it. Tidy your desk, return borrowed items, and identify the best way to handle confidential documents.

- Badges and other forms of security clearance typically need to be returned

- Sensitive documents should be returned to your manager or team members
- Return company laptop, charges, mouse, and other cables in a neat manner

Return Offers

Depending on the company, you may be considered for a return offer at the company. If you do receive one, congratulations, that certainly opens your options. If you do not receive one, which often happens due to financial considerations, company needs, and general fit, do not fret as the experience you have had the last few months will be enough to leverage other opportunities for you.

Hopefully this internship has given you some perspective on whether this is the right industry for you. If it is the right one, look into the return offer to see if the position specifically entails the work you want to be doing in your industry. If not, return to the company, and see if you could negotiate an offer for a different position. If it isn't, take what you have learned, and continue exploring to see what industry is a better fit.

Do not make the mistake of settling in an industry simply because you have the experience, and you have become comfortable. Yes, having experience in one industry can certainly be leverage more easily for similar opportunities. However, as it was mentioned in the beginning of this process, passion for your work, passion for your career, is crucial for long-term work satisfaction and happiness.

Building your Brand

Starting now, starting with your internship, you are building your professional brand. The value of your brand will depend on the quality of work you bring to the table. As a result, it is crucial that you realize whatever work you produce from this point on needs to be a proper representation of who you are.

- In part, this is your **professional image**. How you act and how you dress in both professional and social settings will contribute to this image.
- **Produce quality work** that demonstrates your abilities. Every assignment is indicative of what kind of person you are.
- **Always exceed expectations**. If you consistently exceed expectations, then you certainly are clearly capable are valuable.
- **Aim for highest evaluation scores**. Make it clear that you plan on not only succeeding, but also thriving. By making your ambitions clear, the work you produce will more likely be recognized.
- **Seek opportunities to maximize your value**. Every person, every human capital, is worth a certain amount, as indicated by pay, colleague respect, and shared opportunities. Take steps to maximize your professional worth. This can be achieved in a variety of ways:

    Greater knowledge and experience will allow you to become more industry proficiency.

    Expanding and developing your relationships will increase the value of your network and subsequent opportunities offered.

    Leadership and teamwork skills will increase the level of responsibility you can manage at a company.

    Always continue working hard, and looking for opportunities to develop yourself.